Rookie Read-About® Science

It Could Still Be Coral

By Allan Fowler

Consultants

Linda Cornwell, Learning Resource Consultant,
Indiana Department of Education

Fay Robinson, Child Development Specialist

Lynne Kepler, Educational Consultant

ᑫᑭ Children's Press®
A Division of Grolier Publishing
New York   London   Hong Kong   Sydney
Danbury, Connecticut

Project Editor: Downing Publishing Services
Designer: Herman Adler Design Group
Photo Researcher: Caroline Anderson

Library of Congress Cataloging-in-Publication Data

Fowler, Allan.
    It could still be coral / by Allan Fowler.
      p. cm. – (Rookie read-about science)
    Includes index.
    Summary: Describes the physical characteristics and behavior of coral
polyps and describes what coral reefs are like and how they form.
    ISBN 0-516-20028-3 (lib. bdg.) — ISBN 0-516-26082-0 (pbk.)
    1. Corals—Juvenile literature. 2. Coral reefs and islands—
Juvenile literature. [1. Corals. 2. Coral reefs and islands.] I. Title.
II. Series
QL377.C5F68   1996   98-17570
                                             CIP
                                             AC

Here are some
pieces of coral.

Would you say that coral
is animal or mineral?
In a way, it is both.

Coral is found in the sea. It is made of rock called limestone, and comes in many shapes and colors.

But coral could be an animal — and still be coral.

The coral made of limestone comes from the coral that is an animal. So they are both called coral.

Coral animals are also known as polyps. They live in the ocean, in warm parts of the world.

Most polyps are very small,
less than one inch long.
Their bodies are like jelly.

These polyps are called
stony polyps. They have
hard limestone skeletons.
Your skeleton is inside
your body.

But the skeletons of stony polyps are outside their bodies. These skeletons, piled on top of each other, become coral reefs or coral islands.

There are many different
kinds of stony polyps,
each with a different
shape of skeleton.

Coral could look like
the branches of a tree . . .
the antlers of a deer . . .

the pipes of an organ . . .
mushrooms, leaves of lettuce,

or an open fan . . .
and still be coral.

It could be almost any
color, and still be coral.

Stony polyps gather into large groups, or colonies. Over a long, long time, as the polyps in a colony die, their skeletons may form a ridge, or coral reef.

A reef is made up of
millions of coral skeletons.
The top of a coral reef may
be just below the surface
of the water.

Or it may stick up out of
the water. Some islands
are really coral reefs.

Reefs often form close to
a seashore, or around an
island. Coral reefs form
in warm ocean waters.

By far the largest coral
reef is the Great Barrier
Reef. It stretches for
about 1,250 miles off
the coast of Australia.

Coral reefs are great places to look at marine life.

You can swim, snorkel or scuba dive, or travel in a glass-bottomed boat . . .

and see tropical fish all around you, in every color of the rainbow.

21

Giant clams and
other shellfish . . .
huge sea turtles . . .

underwater animals that
look more like plants . . .
all make their home
among coral reefs.

Birds nest on coral islands.

The coral rock itself
takes many strange
and beautiful forms.

It might look like the inside of a church . . .

or like a garden of brightly colored plants . . .

and still be coral.

And for this underwater world of wonder, we can thank those tiny polyps!

Words You Know

stony polyps

coral reef

Great Barrier Reef, Australia

shellfish

sea turtle

scuba

snorkel

Index

About the Author

Allan Fowler is a free-lance writer with a background in advertising. Born in New York, he lives in Chicago now and enjoys traveling.

Photo Credits

SuperStock International, Inc. — ©Chris Newbert, cover, 4; ©D. J. Meeks, 10

Photo Researchers, Inc. — ©Harry Rogers, 3; ©Nancy Sefton, 6, 27; ©Andrew J. Martinez, 9, 25; ©Fred McConnaughey, 12; ©B. Hunter, 15; ©Takeshi Takahara, 18; ©C. Seghers, 19, 30 (bottom); ©Gregory Ochocki, 22, 31 (top right); ©Andrew G. Weed, 23; ©Chet Tussey/Gregory Ochocki Productions, 28; ©J.W. Mowbrey, 31 (top left)

Visuals Unlimited — ©Dave B. Fleetham, Marine Photographer, 7, 21, 31 (bottom left); ©Don W. Fawcett, 8, 30 (top left); ©W. Ober, 11

Valan Photos — ©Fred Bavendam, 13, 14, 30 (top right); ©Dr. A. Farquhar, 24

Norbert Wu — ©Norbert Wu, 16, 31 (bottom right); ©Roy Smathers/ Mo Yung Productions, 17

COVER: A coral reef on Fiji, South Pacific